by Ellen Lawrence

Consultants:

Suzy Gazlay, MA
Recipient, Presidential Award for Excellence in Science Teaching

Kimberly Brenneman, PhD
National Institute for Early Education Research, Rutgers University, New Brunswick, New Jersey

New York, New York

Credits

Cover, © Paul Maguire/Shutterstock, and © Sura Nualpradid/Shutterstock; 2–3, © CoraMax/Shutterstock, © design56/Shutterstock, © TigerForce/Shutterstock, and © design56/Shutterstock; 3, © CoraMax/Shutterstock and © iStock/Thinkstock; 4, © Menno Schaefer/Shutterstock, © Tatyana Vyc/Shutterstock, © wavebreakmedia/Shutterstock, and © Eric Isselee/Shutterstock; 5, © CoraMax/Shutterstock, © artiomp/Shutterstock, © oksana2010/Shutterstock, and © cristovao/Shutterstock; 6–7, © CoraMax/Shutterstock, © studioVin/Shutterstock, and © iStock/Thinkstock; 8, © Jacopin/Science Photo Library; 8–9, © CoraMax/Shutterstock, and © Coprid/Shutterstock; 9, © Ruby Tuesday Books; 10, © Coprid/Shutterstock; 10–11, © CoraMax/Shutterstock, © SmileStudio/Shutterstock, and © studioVin/Shutterstock; 12, © Ilona Baha/Shutterstock and © Danny Smythe/Shutterstock; 12–13, © CoraMax/Shutterstock, © Piotr Krzeslak/Shutterstock, and © Palo_ok/Shutterstock; 13, © Igor Kovalchuk/Shutterstock; 14, © S.Dashkevych/Shutterstock; 14–15, © Refat/Shutterstock, © Kim Nguyen/Shutterstock, and © Horiyan/Shutterstock; 15, © Marco Mayer/Shutterstock and © CoraMax/Shutterstock; 16–17, © CoraMax/Shutterstock and © vetkit/Shutterstock; 17, © iStock/Thinkstock; 18, © Kamonrat/Shutterstock, © Andrey Arkusha/Shutterstock, © photosync/Shutterstock, © studioVin/Shutterstock, © cenap refik ongan/Shutterstock, © TigerForce/Shutterstock, © Coprid/Shutterstock, and © Ruby Tuesday Books; 18–19, © CoraMax/Shutterstock; 19, © design56/Shutterstock, © TigerForce/Shutterstock, © Igor Kovalchuk/Shutterstock, and © Maen CG/Shutterstock; 20, © Coprid/Shutterstock, © Ruby Tuesday Books, © Smile Studio/Shutterstock, and © studioVin/Shutterstock; 20–21, © CoraMax/Shutterstock and © Paul Maguire/Shutterstock; 21, © Palo_ok/Shutterstock and © dslaven/Shutterstock; 22, © Gelpi JM/Shutterstock, © Evgeniy Moroz/Shutterstock, © ffolas/Shutterstock, © Superstock, © claudiofichera/Shutterstock, and © Lev A./Shutterstock; 23, © CoraMax/Shutterstock, © Jacopin/Science Photo Library, © Pavel L Photo and Video/Shutterstock, © Andrey N. Bannov/Shutterstock, © Alexey V. Smirnov/Shutterstock, and © 2xSamara.com/Shutterstock; 24, © CoraMax/Shutterstock.

Publisher: Kenn Goin
Senior Editor: Joyce Tavolacci
Creative Director: Spencer Brinker
Design: Emma Randall
Photo Researcher: Ruby Tuesday Books Ltd.

Library of Congress Cataloging-in-Publication Data

Lawrence, Ellen, 1967– author.
  Sound / by Ellen Lawrence ; consultants, Suzy Gazlay, MA recipient, Presidential Award for Excellence in Science Teaching ; Kimberly Brenneman, PhD National Institute for Early Education Research, Rutgers University, New Brunswick, New Jersey.
     pages cm. — (FUN-damental experiments)
  Includes bibliographical references and index.
  ISBN-13: 978-1-62724-094-9 (library binding)
  ISBN-10: 1-62724-094-2 (library binding)
  1. Sound—Juvenile literature. 2. Sound—Experiments—Juvenile literature. I. Title. II. Series: Lawrence, Ellen, 1967– FUNdamental experiments.
  QC225.5.L39 2014
  534.078—dc23
                                   2013041513

For more information, write to Bearport Publishing Company, Inc., 45 West 21st Street, Suite 3B, New York, NY 10010. Printed in the United States of America.

10 9 8 7 6 5 4 3 2 1

Contents

Let's Investigate Sound

Music, laughter, a dog barking—every day, your world is filled with sound. Sound is a type of **energy** that is made when the air **vibrates**. You can't see the air vibrating, but your ears pick up the vibrations and allow you to hear sound. Inside this book are lots of fun experiments and amazing facts about sound. So grab a notebook, and let's start exploring!

Check It Out!

If you pluck the strings of a guitar, you can see the strings move, or vibrate. The vibration of the strings makes the air vibrate, which creates sound. The vibrations from the guitar's strings travel in waves through the air. They travel away from the guitar in every direction. You can't see the waves of sound, but they act just like waves in water do. Let's check it out.

- Fill a shallow bowl with water.
- Drop a small stone into the center of the bowl.
- Do you see the waves traveling through the water away from the pebble?

Sound waves in the air act just like the waves in the water.

What makes a sound loud or quiet?

Not all sounds are the same. Some are loud and some are soft. Let's investigate how different sounds are made.

You will need:

- A large rubber band
- A small plastic bowl
- A notebook and pencil

1 Stretch a rubber band around a bowl. It should be stretched across the top and under the bottom of the bowl.

▶ What do you think the rubber band will do if you pluck, or pull, it?

Write your **prediction** in your notebook.

2 Now test your prediction by plucking the rubber band.

▶ Does your prediction match what happened?

3 Try plucking the rubber band very gently.

▶ What do you see and hear?

▶ What do you think will happen if you pluck the rubber band much harder?

Write down your prediction.

4 Pluck the rubber band harder.

▶ Does your prediction match what happened?

Record in your notebook everything that happened.

▶ What created the noises you heard?

▶ How did the different vibrations make different sounds?

▶ What kind of vibrations made quiet sounds?

▶ What kind of vibrations made loud sounds?

(To learn more about this investigation and find the answers to the questions, see pages 20–21.)

7

How do ears work?

As sound waves travel through the air, they enter your ear and travel down a tube called an ear canal until they reach your **eardrum**. An eardrum is a piece of skin that's tightly stretched across the ear canal. The sound waves cause the eardrum to vibrate, sending the waves deeper into your ear. Here, the vibrations touch tiny hairs that send signals to your brain, which turns the signals into sounds that you hear. Let's investigate how this works.

You will need:

- Plastic wrap
- A ceramic bowl
- A pan lid
- A metal spoon
- Some sugar
- A notebook and pencil

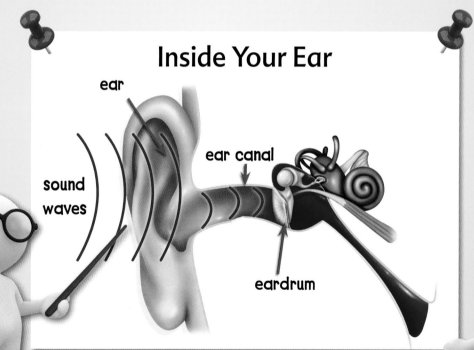

Inside Your Ear

ear

ear canal

sound waves

eardrum

1 To make a model of an eardrum, tightly stretch some plastic wrap over the top of a bowl.

2 Hold a pan lid about six inches (15 cm) from the bowl. Bang the lid with the spoon. As you do this, watch the model eardrum.

▶ What do you think happened when you banged the pan lid?

▶ Could you see the model eardrum vibrating?

3 Now place some sugar on the model eardrum.

▶ What do you think will happen to the sugar when you bang the pan lid?

Write your prediction in your notebook.

4 Now bang the pan lid again.

▶ What did you observe happening?

▶ What do you think made the sugar act as it did?

Record in your notebook everything that happened.

▶ When you banged the pan lid, you couldn't see the sound waves. How did you know they were there?

(To learn more about this investigation and find the answers to the questions, see pages 20–21.)

What makes a sound high-pitched or low-pitched?

You've already discovered that weak vibrations make quiet noises and strong vibrations make loud noises. The loudness of a noise is called its **volume**. A noise also has a **pitch**. Some noises, like a squeaky dog toy, are high-pitched. Other noises, like the rumble of thunder, are low-pitched. Let's investigate how vibrations can make noises sound high or low.

You will need:

- A long rubber band
- A ruler
- A pencil
- A notebook and another pencil

1 Stretch a rubber band lengthwise over a ruler.

2 Slide a pencil under the rubber band about two inches (5 cm) from the ruler's end.

rubber band

3 Hold the ruler with one hand and pluck the middle of the long section of the rubber band with your other hand.

▶ What sound do you hear?

▶ What kind of noise do you think you will hear if you pluck the short section of the rubber band?

4 Now pluck the middle of the short section of the rubber band.

▶ Does this noise sound higher or lower than the first noise?

5 Try moving the pencil to different positions on the ruler, and then pluck the rubber band.

▶ How does the sound change in each position?

▶ What do you notice about the rubber band when it makes a high-pitched sound?

▶ What do you notice about the rubber band when it makes a low-pitched sound?

(To learn more about this investigation and find the answers to the questions, see pages 20–21.)

Can you make sounds with different pitches?

In the last investigation, you discovered that noises can be high-pitched or low-pitched. In this activity, you are going to use glasses of water to make sounds that have different pitches. Let's investigate!

- Five glasses
- A jug of water
- A teaspoon
- A notebook and pencil

1 Line up five glasses. Pour about one inch (2.5 cm) of water into the first glass. Fill the second glass nearly to the top.

2 Then pour different amounts of water into the last three glasses.

3 Use a spoon to gently tap the side of the glass that has the least amount of water.

 5 Arrange the glasses so they are in order from the lowest pitched to the highest pitched. Try playing a tune using the glasses as instruments!

▶ Did the glass make a high-pitched or low-pitched sound?

▶ What kind of sound do you think the glass that's nearly full will make? What about the other glasses?

 4 Write your predictions in your notebook, and then test them.

▶ Do your predictions match what happened?

Record in your notebook everything you observed.

▶ What could you do to change the sound of the glass that has the most water?

▶ Why do you think the glasses make different sounds?

(To learn more about this investigation and find the answers to the questions, see pages 20-21.)

Can sound waves travel through objects?

You've heard lots of sounds made by vibrations traveling through air. In this next investigation, we're going to find out if it's possible for sound waves to travel through **solid** objects, such as string or metal. Before beginning the investigation, make your own prediction and write it in your notebook. Now, let's investigate!

You will need:

- A piece of string about 18 inches (46 cm) long
- A wire coat hanger
- A table
- A notebook and pencil

1 Tie the center of a piece of string around the hook of a coat hanger.

2 Ask an adult to loosely tie each end of the string around each of your index fingers, so you are holding the coat hanger by two fingers.

3 Gently swing the coat hanger and tap it against the top of the table.

▶ Describe what the noise sounds like.

▶ Was it a loud or quiet noise?

Untie your fingers and write your observations in your notebook.

4 Now have an adult loosely tie the string around your fingers again. This time put your fingers in your ears, then gently tap the coat hanger against the table.

▶ What does the noise sound like now?

▶ How does it compare to the first noise?

Record in your notebook everything that happened.

▶ How was it possible for the sound of the coat hanger tapping on the table to travel up the string and through your fingers?

▶ Was the sound louder when it traveled through air or through solids?

▶ Did your observations match your first prediction?

(To learn more about this investigation and find the answers to the questions, see pages 20–21.)

What happens when sound waves are captured?

When an object vibrates and makes noise, sound waves travel away from the object in all directions. If those sound waves are weak, the noise will be quiet and difficult to hear. What happens if the sound waves are made to travel in one direction? Let's investigate!

You will need:

- A large piece of construction paper
- A pair of scissors
- Tape
- A radio or other device for playing music
- A notebook and pencil

1 Roll a piece of paper into a cone that's about 12 inches (30.5 cm) long. The narrow opening should be about the size of a quarter.

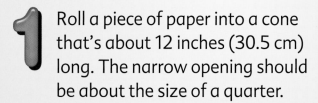

2 Trim the wide opening of the cone so that it is flat and can stand upright on a table.

3 Put the cone down and turn on a radio. Set the volume very low.

4 Sit with your ear about 12 inches (30.5 cm) from the radio's speaker.

▶ How well can you hear the radio?

Give the sound a score from one to ten, with one being very difficult to hear and ten being easy to hear. Write the score in your notebook.

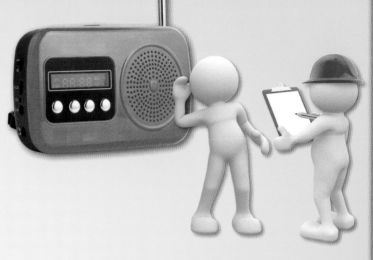

5 Now pick up your cone and hold it so the wide opening is against the radio's speaker and the narrow opening is just touching your ear.

▶ How well can you hear the radio now?

▶ What score would you give the sound?

Record in your notebook everything that happened.

▶ Were the sounds that traveled through the cone easier or harder to hear?

▶ Why do you think that is?

(To learn more about this investigation and find the answers to the questions, see pages 20–21.)

Can you invent a musical instrument?

You've discovered that you can make sounds by plucking a rubber band, hitting a pan lid, and tapping containers of water. Now try using what you've learned about vibrations and sound to invent your own musical instrument!

You will need:

- Your choice of materials to make an instrument, such as a paper towel tube, a spoon, metal or plastic containers, boxes, glass jars, string, rubber bands, and beads
- A notebook and pencil

1 Before you get started, here are some ideas to think about.

▸ How will your instrument vibrate, or make sound?

▸ Does your instrument have a part that can be plucked?

▸ Will it make loud noises, soft noises, or both?

▶ Will your instrument vibrate if you hit it?

▶ Will your instrument make a noise when you shake it?

 Start by drawing a picture of your instrument in your notebook.

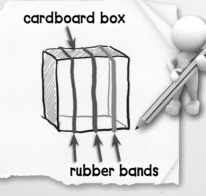

cardboard box

rubber bands

 Collect the materials you need, and get building!

In your notebook, describe your instrument and how it works. Try answering these questions. The answers will help you write your description.

▶ How do you make your instrument vibrate?

▶ Where do the vibrations come from?

▶ Can your instrument be played both quietly and loudly? How?

▶ Does your instrument make high-pitched sounds, low-pitched sounds, or both? Why do you think this is?

(To learn more about this investigation and find the answers to the questions, see pages 20–21.)

Discovery Time

It's fun to investigate sound in our world. Now let's check out all the exciting things we've discovered.

What makes a sound loud or quiet?

Pages 6-7

When you plucked the rubber band, it vibrated. The rubber band's vibrations made the air vibrate, which made a twang sound.

Gently plucking the rubber band made a quiet sound. Plucking the rubber band harder made a louder sound. That's because weak vibrations make quiet sounds and strong vibrations make louder sounds.

How do ears work?

Pages 8-9

Banging the pan lid made it vibrate. These vibrations made the air vibrate, causing sound waves to hit the model eardrum.

Vibrations in the air made the model eardrum vibrate. It's very difficult to see the plastic wrap on the model eardrum vibrating, though. When you placed sugar on the plastic wrap, however, you could see the sugar move around. This showed that the model eardrum was vibrating and the vibrations were moving the sugar.

The sound waves also made your actual eardrums vibrate. This allowed you to hear the banging noise.

What makes a sound high-pitched or low-pitched?

Pages 10-11

Short objects make fast vibrations that are high-pitched, while long objects make slower vibrations that are low-pitched. When you plucked the short section of the rubber band, it vibrated fast because it was stretched tight. As a result, it made a high-pitched sound.

The longer section of the rubber band was not only longer but it was stretched less tight. As a result, it vibrated more slowly and made a lower-pitched sound.

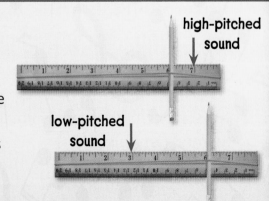

high-pitched sound

low-pitched sound

20

Can you make sounds with different pitches?

The glass that contained the least water vibrated quickly when you tapped it, so it made a high-pitched sound. The glass that was nearly full vibrated more slowly, so it made a lower-pitched sound when you tapped it. If you remove some water from a full glass, it will vibrate faster and make a higher-pitched sound. Adding water to a glass makes it vibrate more slowly and lowers its sound.

Pages 12-13

low-pitched sound   high-pitched sound

Can sound waves travel through objects?

When you first tapped the coat hanger on the table, it made sound waves. You heard these sound waves move through the air. When you put your fingers in your ears and tapped the hanger again, you could hear the sound waves moving through solids. They traveled from the coat hanger, up the string, through your fingers, and into your ears.

The noise probably sounded louder when it traveled through solids. That's because sound waves travel better through solids than through air.

Pages 14-15

What happens when sound waves are captured?

The weak sound waves coming from the radio spread out across the room so they were difficult to hear.

The paper cone captured the sound waves and forced them to travel in one direction toward your ear. This made the sound waves easier to hear.

Pages 16-17

Can you invent a musical instrument?

Different instruments make sounds in different ways. For example, a guitar's strings are plucked to make them vibrate. The stretched skin of a drum is hit to make it vibrate. Think about what part of your instrument vibrates to make sound.

When an instrument makes weak vibrations, it makes quiet sounds. Stronger vibrations make louder sounds.

A high-pitched sound comes from an instrument that is vibrating fast. A deep or low-pitched sound comes from an instrument that is vibrating slowly.

Pages 18-19

21

Sound in Your World

Now that you've discovered a lot about this amazing type of energy, start investigating the sounds around you.

1. Sit quietly indoors or outdoors and listen for sounds.

▶ **How many different sounds can you hear? List them in your notebook. What do all the sounds have in common?**

2. Gently place your fingertips on your throat. Now shout your name. Next, say your name as if speaking normally. Then whisper your name.

▶ **What do your fingertips feel each time? What do you think is happening?**

3. Open a window and listen to the sounds outside. Now carefully shut the window.

▶ **What do you notice about the sounds?**

4. Sometimes, you can hear a noise even if it's far away from you. For example, you can hear a fire truck's siren when it's many blocks away.

▶ **What do you notice about the truck's siren as it gets nearer to you?**

Answers: 1. All the sounds are made by vibrations, or sound waves, that travel through the air and into your ear. 2. When you talk, body parts in your throat called vocal cords create sound waves. You hear these sound waves as your voice. When you shout, your vocal cords make strong vibrations. When you whisper, they make gentle vibrations. 3. The window is blocking sound waves coming from outside. Solids may block sound waves completely or allow some sound waves to travel through. 4. A fire truck's siren sounds quiet when it's far away. That's because sound waves get weaker the farther they have to travel. When the fire truck gets close, however, the vibrations reach your ears at full strength, so the siren sounds very loud.

Science Words

eardrum (*ihr*-druhm) a piece of skin inside the ear that is tightly stretched across a tube called the ear canal; when sound waves hit the eardrum, it vibrates, making it possible to hear sounds

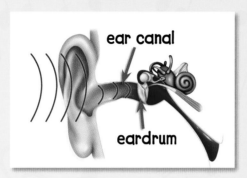

ear canal

eardrum

energy (EN-ur-jee) a power that can come from different sources; for example, sound waves made by a vibrating object

pitch (PICH) how high or low a sound is; for example, a whistle makes a high-pitched sound while the sound of a dump truck's engine is low-pitched

prediction (pri-DIK-shuhn) a guess that something will happen in a certain way; a prediction is often based on facts a person knows or something a person has observed

solid (SOL-id) a material that has a definite size and shape, such as wood and metal

vibrates (*vye*-brates) moves back and forth

volume (VOL-yuhm) how quiet or loud a sound is

high-pitched

low-pitched

23

Index

Read More

Ballard, Carol. *Exploring Sound (How Does Science Work?).* New York: PowerKids Press (2008).

Guillain, Charlotte. *Different Sounds.* Chicago: Heinemann (2009).

Owen, Ruth. *My Amazing Sense of Hearing (My Body: Inside and Out).* New York: Ruby Tuesday Books (2014).

Learn More Online

To learn more about sound, visit
www.bearportpublishing.com/FundamentalExperiments

About the Author

Ellen Lawrence lives in the United Kingdom. Her favorite books to write are those about nature and animals. In fact, the first book Ellen bought for herself, when she was six years old, was the story of a gorilla named Patty Cake that was born in New York's Central Park Zoo.